SOCIAL ISSUES, JUSTICE AND STATUS

# SOCIAL NETWORKING AND THE LIBRARIES IN THE NEW MILLENNIUM

## AN ANNOTATED BIBLIOGRAPHY

# SOCIAL ISSUES, JUSTICE AND STATUS

Additional books in this series can be found on Nova's website under the Series tab.

Additional E-books in this series can be found on Nova's website under the E-book tab.

SOCIAL ISSUES, JUSTICE AND STATUS

# SOCIAL NETWORKING AND THE LIBRARIES IN THE NEW MILLENNIUM

## AN ANNOTATED BIBLIOGRAPHY

DEVA ESWARA REDDY

**Nova Science Publishers, Inc.**
*New York*

For permission to use material from this book please contact us:
Telephone 631-231-7269; Fax 631-231-8175
Web Site: http://www.novapublishers.com



**LIBRARY OF CONGRESS CATALOGING-IN-PUBLICATION DATA**

Eswara Reddy, Deva B., compiler.
Social networking and the libraries in the new millennium : an annotated bibliography / [compiled by] Deva Eswara Reddy.
pages cm
Includes bibliographical references and indexes.
ISBN 978-1-62081-758-2
1. Online social networks--Library applications--Bibliography. I. Title.
Z674.75.S63E89 2012
302.30285--dc23
2012013602

*Published by Nova Science Publishers, Inc. † New York*

*I dedicate this book to my wife*

*Prabhavathi*

# Contents

# PREFACE

Social networking is a hackneyed phrase used day in and day out. It is said that social networking has been around for a long time, as early as the time of Plato in 400 B.C., when scholars and philosophers studied and analyzed the formation and interaction of groups of people. However, the advent of the Internet and the online social networking phenomenon has revolutionized the communication process among one to one or one-to-many interactions with known and unknown folks across time and space. Online social networking has branched off to over 350 sites such as Facebook, MySpace, Twitter, LinkedIn, and Academia. It may not be an exaggeration if one says that social networking is omnipresent and all pervasive regardless of age, geographical location, profession, and occupation. It is present in every community, irrespective of political or religious beliefs; it is a tool being used universally for reaching a wider audience than any other media. The emergence of these digital media has blurred traditional acceptance of private and public spheres where a part of our daily routine life takes place. Incidentally, most online social networking sites have emerged in the New Millennium. Recognizing that over 85% of college students use one or the other social networking sites, libraries and higher education in general aim at going to the students where they are or offer resources and services in the media most commonly used by students. An increasing number of college and university libraries have embraced social networking sites as a tool to promote services, provide information, and offer instruction.

It is noteworthy that the terms "social media" and "social networking" are in use synonymously. Nevertheless, they refer to different contexts. Social media is a system that disseminates information to others. On the other hand, social networking is a tool for connecting, depending on the topic or subject matter. In other words, through social networking, relationships or connections are developed. Many a time the terms social media and social networking are in use interchangeably.

Libraries and librarians are evincing great interest in social networking as a tool for teaching and outreach. Although library and information science schools have shown some interest in social networking, this phenomenon has not made any inroads into the course content of library schools such as cataloging, indexing, and reference service. Libraries and librarians are finding that used properly it can be a great tool to save time and money to promote library services and collections.

This publication focuses on finding current trends in the use of social networking in libraries in the New Millennium. A review of literature on social networking, more specifically, searching of databases such as *LISA: Library and Information Science Abstracts, Library Literature & Information Science Full Text*, and *Google Scholar* reveals about 1000 articles and other materials of general nature of which several articles, reports, and books deal with libraries.

This annotated bibliography documents the role of social networking sites in all types of libraries such as school, college, university, public, special, and community libraries in the New Millennium covering the period 2000-2011. Each analyzed entry highlights the usefulness of the article. Highlighted aspects of social networks include teens and young adults, privacy and trust, behavioral and social sciences, health sciences, and the role of US Congress. This handy reference work and the literature it covers would enable libraries and decision makers to plan on how they can adopt social networking sites and for what ends, how much time and effort one should invest in these platforms, and how to monitor their success. Title, author, and subject indexes are an added pathway to the users of this book.

ACKNOWLEDGMENTS

I would like to thank Mr. Jonathan Marner for editorial help provided to me.

I thank my son Shivakumar Reddy and daughter Geetha Baddigam for their assistance.

# ANNOTATED BIBLIOGRAPHY

Agosto, D. E., & Abbas, J. (2009).Teens and social networking: How public libraries are responding to the latest online trend. *Public Libraries,* 48(3), 32-37. Noticing the growing use of social networking sites among teens, this paper reviews the research related to adolescents' use of social networking utilities. The authors show how public libraries have responded to the trend and argue that social networking tools can be beneficial both to public libraries that serve teens and to their adolescent patrons as well. Several pertinent questions discussed include the reasons for teens using social networking utilities, how wide spread is the social networking trend among teens, why public libraries use social networking utilities, and how have public libraries responded to the social networking trend in promoting teens' online safety. The author says that by adapting social networking public libraries can benefit in a number of ways such as broadening the reach of the library's young adult programs and services, enabling the library to better support teens' healthy social development; and facilitating opportunities for public librarians to teach teens how to engage in safer online interactions.

Ahmadi, S. (2012).The effect of social online networking service on public libraries via critical systems heuristics (CSH): A case study. *International Journal of Computer & Communication Technology*, 3, (2) 50-54. This article aims at discussing the impact of social online networking on library services by a qualitative evaluation method. The author reviews literature on the concepts of Web 2.0 and library 2.0 and evaluates the use of Facebook as a Web 2.0 technology tool by a method that was introduced by Werner Ulrich in 1983 under the term Critical Systems Heuristics (CSH).CSH is a framework for reflective practice based on practical, philosophical, and systems thinking. The author chooses Kansas City Public Library for this case study and applies CSH's framework of "boundary categories" that translates into a checklist of twelve critical boundary questions, broadly under client beneficiary's role, decision maker's role, and expertise's role. This paper aims at studying the effect of Facebook in establishing connections between staff and users, communication between users and users, and staff with staff to share information and to market library services.

Aharony, N. (2010). Twitter use in libraries: An exploratory analysis. *Journal of WebLibrarianship,* 4(4), 333-350. Twitter is an online social networking service that enables its user to read text-based messages up to 140 characters known as "tweets". Twitter is a microblogging service while Facebook has many features including a microblogging component. Based on an extensive review of the literature, this paper provides a basic understanding of Twitter, tweets, and the scope of tweets. Aimed at finding the benefits of Twitter in academic and public libraries, the study seeks answers to quantitative difference in tweets produced, the linguistic difference in tweets created, and the difference in the content of the tweets produced by academic and public libraries. The research findings based on the statistical analysis and content analysis show that there are some differences between public and academic libraries. The paper concludes that using Twitter in libraries enables both kinds of libraries to broadcast and share information about their activities, opinions, status, and professional interests. The author says that the findings are relevant for librarians and information scientists to better understand and explore the phenomenon of library tweets.

ALA (2010). *State of America's libraries report - Social networking and libraries Section.* Retrieved on 2/25/2012, from http://www.ala.org/news/mediapresscenter/americaslibraries/socialnetworking. The state of America's libraries report commissioned by the American Library Association comments on social networking and other issues of concern for libraries, including library funding, library technology, construction and renovation, outreach, and diversity. The report, based on a survey of more than 900 library administrators/managers, librarians and other staff, indicates that many libraries are making good use of social media and Web 2.0 applications. The report, which was based on a separate study, ranks Facebook as the runaway winner when respondents were asked to choose from a list of 25 Web 2.0 and social media tools their library uses. The top three tools are: Facebook, at 84.3 percent; Twitter 49.2 percent; and Blogging tools, 42.4 percent; This report in summary says that U.S.libraries of all types continue to make increasing use of social media and Web 2.0 applications and tools to connect with library users and to market programs and services. The section on social networking, as well as other sections, is very informative for professionals as well as for general information to the library lovers.

Alayo, A. (2009). The presence of libraries on Facebook. *Impact: Journal of the CareerDevelopment Group,* 12 (4), 96-97. This is an anecdotal article mentioning how the author began familiarizing herself with the social network site Facebook in order to keep in touch with her colleagues and friends whom she has not seen or spoken for several years. She says that libraries are making their presence felt on Facebook to take advantage of its popularity among the student community. The author observes that Facebook pages maintained by libraries are used for posting library information such as opening hours, contact information, library links, subject guides, catalog and database search functions, and chat applications. One of the main obstacles she finds is that Facebook does not allow the organizations to register and the page is tied to the person who creates it. She feels that since the younger generation and students are addicted to social networking, libraries should see this as an opportunity to reach out to them.

Albanese, A. R. (2006). Google is not the net: Social networks are surging and present the real service challenge--and opportunity--for libraries. *Library Journal,* 131(15), 32. This paper starts by saying that that the presence of social networks sites is also posing a challenge as well as opportunities for library services. At the same time Google's ubiquitous presence is also a bit troubling. Based on his observation at American Library Association (ALA) annual conference in New Orleans, the author says that Google hardly plays down those fears. He narrates the reactions of various librarians at the conference and asks the librarians not to be scared of Google and other commercial search firms, as the goals and objectives of libraries are entirely different. He says that Google is pervasive in many realms that used to be specifically what libraries did. It is the collection; the way of searching and the navigation mechanism that Google adopts that makes it seemingly unique. The author appeals to librarians not to be myopic when it comes to Google. The Web evolves and new opportunities and challenges emerge larger for libraries than who's capturing the bulk of the search or email markets, or who's giving us driving directions. He concludes by saying that no one comes to libraries to search and contact us for learning, community, and other services.

Axelsson, A. (2008). Libraries, social community sites and Facebook. *Scandinavian Public Library Quarterly,* September. pp. 18-19. The author recognizes the value and benefits of Facebook to libraries in Sweden and explores the role libraries could have in Facebook and similar communities. She starts with the basic question about the relevancy of Facebook for libraries and concedes that libraries can target several aspects of Facebook to benefit from it and observes Facebook as a useful tool for both public and academic libraries. She says that students constitute the largest member group in Facebook and more than every other 20-30 year old in Sweden is a Facebook member. An important characteristic of Facebook is that information spreads virally, i.e. with word of mouth. However, she adds that this type of application does not really create any special activity allowing comparison with others. She foresees limited use of Facebook for libraries.

Balas, J. L. (2008) Social networks and the library community. *Computers in Libraries,* 28(4), 40. This article says that all types of libraries - public, academic, school, or special or community libraries - are using social networking sites because each one serves a specific community. She explains that public libraries generally serve geographic communities, and academic and school libraries serve institutional communities, while special libraries serve corporate communities.

She opines that the library building has often served as a physical center of its community, but now that resources are accessible without visiting the library building, librarians are creating social networks to foster the sense of community among library users. This column under the title Online Treasures reports and lists various useful online resources such as blogs, announcements and articles with their URLs.

Barack, L. (2009). School librarians lead in social networking. *School Library Journal,* 55 (12), 17. This is a summary of a survey--cosponsored by edWeb.net, a social networking site for educators and MCH Inc. According to this survey, media specialists are more likely to join social networking sites than teachers and principals--and they are more likely to adopt a variety of content-sharing tools for personal, professional, and classroom use. The report further says that the teachers are fully aware that students use this technology every day and believe they need it for success in life, but lack time to use these tools in the classroom. School librarians are most positive about the value of social networking in education, but are disappointed with their districts blocking access to Web sites like YouTube and Facebook. Facebook was the most popular site for educators followed by MySpace and LinkedIn. Educators used these sites mainly to connect with family and friends.

Bodnar, J., & Doshi, A. (2011).Asking the right questions: A critique of Facebook, social media, and libraries. *Public Services Quarterly,* 7(3-4), 102-110. The authors of this paper, based on their professional experience using Facebook, Twitter and other social networking sites, as well as their review of library literature on these sites, and their discussions with librarians about these tools, offer a critique of these tools. They notice in the literature either positive or negative assessments of the sites and of their potential use for academic libraries. The positive comments appear to be over simplistic glorifying computerization as the panacea for all the good things in the world. The negative comments in the literature on Facebook and other social networking sites often fear librarians overstepping their bounds with library users. The authors encourage librarians and others to think more deeply about the use of social networking sites in their libraries while critically examining sites themselves and what others have said and written about them. The authors suggest questions and directions for future practitioners and researchers.

Breeding, M. (2007). Librarians face online social networks. *Computers in Libraries,* 27(8), 30-32. This introductory article recognizes that the emergence of online social networking is suddenly attracting Web users of all generations. Examples of tools include sites such as MySpace, Facebook, LinkedIn, and Friendster ranking among the most popular. The author sketches out some of the basic features of Facebook to help kindle interest in it. The author wishes that librarians take a closer look at Facebook and explore some of the ways it might make a difference for them working in libraries. He mentions the key role-played in academic libraries and in the lives of student clientele including high school students, and further recognizes that many in the library profession have discovered Facebook as a well-suited tool for developing their own social and professional networks online. The author asks librarians to join the Facebook to learn and explore the versatility of it themselves. This paper foresees several options and opportunities in using Facebook as a venue for the library's outreach to students and visualizes librarians answering late night questions ranging from trivia to last-minute information emergencies.

Breeding, M. (2009). Social Networking Strategies for Professionals. *Computers in Libraries*, 29(9), 29-31. This author says that social networking brings a new dimension to the professional lives of those involved with libraries and encourages librarians and information professionals to use social networking sites so that they can enrich their knowledge and skills as well as provide up-to-date service to patrons. The author focuses on Facebook, LinkedIn, and Twitter and illustrates for what purpose the respective tool helps the librarian. Facebook, despite its popularity among librarians, the author says, is useful mostly for recreational activities. LinkedIn, the author states, fulfills a specialized role as a career-building network and is great in establishing contacts within one's area of specialization as a gateway for emerging software, technologies, and new or interesting ideas or projects. Talking about Twitter at great length, the article describes it as a tool for staying current in the areas of interest such as interesting articles and reports, as well as other literature and Up-to-the-Second News.

Burckhardt, A. (2010). Social media: A guide for college and university Libraries *College & Research Libraries News,* 71(1), 10-12, 24. This paper expects to serve as a practical guide for starting a successful social media presence in academic libraries. Recognizing social media as a powerful form of communication channel growing at exponential rate, the author cites the examples of Facebook and Twitter used by millions of people in their everyday lives for both work and play. The author says that the Facebook and Twitter are well suited for a variety of purposes such as interacting with faculty, staff, and students and for spreading the news about different events or services that they offer as well as to market new library products or initiatives. This article provides practical tips and tricks for college and university libraries on how to launch and sustain a successful social media presence. The author discusses in detail the logistics of launching social media inclusive of preparation work, content creation and management, marketing tips and communication strategies, and feedback.

Burton, J. (2008). UK public libraries and social networking services. *Library Hi Tech News*, 25(4), 5-7 DS is the UK's leading public library management system supplier, and it has recently merged with the Axiell Library Group family of companies. This paper describes how public libraries can gain social networking services for the first time with DS Arena. It provides a description of DS Arena and outlines its potential uses. DS Arena is built on modern foundations, which are critical in service delivery in the rapidly evolving Web 2.0 landscape. It uses a framework of web services to provide content and interactive services. The author says that DS Arena provides a real opportunity for library and information services to deliver services. The paper describes DS as one of the pioneers in the industry in the UK, responsible for a number of innovations in library and archival systems such as library use of barcodes, online circulation systems, hand held devices, secure web browsers, hierarchical database for archives, implementation of RFID in UK libraries, and web-based community information systems.

Carson, B. M. (2010).Libraries and social media. *Information Outlook*, 14(7), 9-12. The author recognizes the impact of social media tools on both the society and on the practice of librarianship. However, he says that social media could be confronted with a variety of legal problems if librarians are not careful in developing and implementing usage policies prior to its adoption. He gives several examples such as copyright violations running to defamation law and disclosure of trade secrets landing in the right of privacy law. He asks librarians to be guarded in blog postings on organization by employees which may expose an organization to liability. Other examples mentioned include, conducting or advertising a promotion on Facebook, misleading advertisements, and broadcast on social media. The author cautions librarians while endorsing user-generated content which may present potential legal pitfalls, since the Federal Trade Commission (FTC) has jurisdiction over false or misleading advertisements. He further says that the existing laws are equally applicable to social media. This is an informative and useful article.

Charnigo, Laurie & Barnett-Ellis, Paula. (2007). Checking Out Facebook.com: The Impact of a Digital Trend on Academic Libraries. *Information Technology and Libraries*, 26(1), 23. This article recognizes the lack of in depth studies on online social networking sites with reference to library and information science. The authors present the findings of a survey of 126 academic librarians, chosen from a random sample of the 850 institutions of higher education in the United States, about their perceptions toward the social network site Facebook focusing on awareness of Facebook, practical impact of the site on library services, and perspectives of librarians toward online social networks. Findings of the survey report reveal that librarians are well aware of the 'Facebook phenomenon'. Those most eager about the potential of online social networking, suggest ideas for using Facebook to promote library services and events. A few librarians notice problems or distractions because of patrons accessing Facebook in the library. In such cases, librarians appear to be not in favor of imposition of strict regulation of access to the Facebook. The authors say that while some librarians are enthusiastic about the possibilities of Facebook, the majority of librarians surveyed appear to consider Facebook outside the purview of professional librarianship.

Chase, D. (2008). Using online social networks, podcasting, and a blog to enhance access to Stony Brook University health sciences library resources and services. *Journal of*

*Electronic Resources in Medical Libraries*, 5(2), 123-132. Based on an OCLC study and a literature review, the authors of this paper observe that very few online users begin their information searching on library web sites and that the majority of users access social networks such as Facebook and MySpace. The authors perceive that for online users, social networks, blogs, and podcasts provide an effective and easy-to-use means for accessing dynamic content and interacting with the library. This article describes methods used by Stony Brook University Health Sciences Library staff to build user communities and to share library resources in online destinations. Other methods adopted by the staff include reference service with instant messaging; utilizing content and link sharing social networking Web sites such as del.icio.us for sharing bookmarks; Flickr for sharing images to connect with users, other libraries and librarians; and podcasting technology to deliver online multimedia learning tools. Other approaches include tagging and developing a WordPress blog to share online tutorials and podcasts, and establishing a Facebook presence.

Chu, M., & Nalani Meulemans, Y. (2008).The problems and potential of MySpace and Facebook usage in academic libraries. *Internet Reference Services Quarterly,* 13(1), 69-85. Noticing the widespread popularity and high ranking traffic figures on the usage of Facbook and MySpace, the authors of this paper aim at finding out as to why Facebook and MySpace are the technology of choice of college students and how these sites are used as channels of communication. In addition, the authors intend to figure out how these technologies are adoptable by libraries and librarians. Based on data from a web-based survey instrument administered to general education course students and focus groups in a college, this paper presents findings of how students are using MySpace and Facebook and discusses how to consider appropriate implementations of MySpace and Facebook in an academic library setting. The possible areas of implementation include content delivery, reference assistance, outreach, and information literacy instruction. The paper points out those students were not particularly interested in using MySpace/Facebook to communicate directly with professors and that students prefer to use emails. The authors suggest that for further studies on these sites should focus at adoption on residential versus commuter campuses as well as differences in adoption by age and degree of adoption.

Clark, J. R. (2008). The Internet connection: Do social networking sites have a place in the behavioral or social science library? *Behavioral & Social Sciences Librarian,* 27(2), 116-118. This short introductory article aims at focusing on the value of social networking for the social science community and describes briefly the salient features of selected social networking sites. For each of the sites, the author provides examples and mentions how the librarian can use these sites effectively for serving patrons. The author describes YouTube as a useful tool for a video pathfinder and for uploading scholarly videos; MySpace as a logging event scheduling facility; Facebook as a tool geared more toward lifestyle and vocational preferences;

Live Journal as a site capable of allowing members to create and post thoughts, opinions, essays, stories, and poetry; and Shelfari.com and LibraryThing.com as useful sites for authors and institutions to share lists of books and discussions on similar topics.

Clay Powers, A. (2008). Social networking as ethical discourse: Blogging a practical and normative library ethic. *Journal of Library Administration,* 47(3-4), 191-209. This paper focuses on the growing need for addressing ethics of librarianship and describes how the library profession has struggled over the last eighty years to define ethics, both through its professional associations and though library literature. The author points out that the codes developed by the American Library Association to guide libraries in their activities are not in a position to address ongoing daily concerns in the profession, as they have become static and the publication schedule in the scholarly literature is not keeping pace with the challenges facing the library profession. She calls for a dynamic, democratic ethical discussion to define a pragmatic ethics that will meet ongoing problems facing libraries. The author opines that social networking tools and blogs in particular, are well suited as the channel for facilitating conversation through the community of contributors and bloggers sharing their values, debating ideals, and creating a forum to address conflicting opinions.

Connell, R. S. (2009). Academic libraries, Facebook and MySpace, and student outreach: A survey of student opinion. *Portal: Libraries and the Academy,* 9(1), 25-36. This paper acknowledges the growing trend in the emergence of new social networking sites and says that the literature related to connecting library users via social networking sites has not addressed the question of interaction between the librarians and college students through Facebook and MySpace. This author surveys 366 undergraduate college students to discover their perceptions in using Facebook and MySpace as outreach tools. The findings reveal that vast majority of respondents had social network profiles and most indicated that they would be accepting of library contact through those Web sites. However, the study shows that a sizable minority responded negatively to this concept. These students, apparently, felt that this potential to infringe upon of their personal privacy.The author asks the librarians to proceed with caution while implementing online social network profiles. Connell concludes this paper by observing that word of mouth would work better as an advertising means via library instruction sessions, freshman orientations, blogs, and the library Web site.

Cooke, N. A. (2008). Social networking in libraries: New tricks of the trade, part I. *Public Services Quarterly, 4*(3), 233-246 and Part II. *Public Services Quarterly*, 4(4), 353-365. This is a very informative two-part collaborative review article, useful for working librarians, focusing on various social networking sites that the librarians can use in better serving the patrons. The author has selected these as examples of social networking sites that have great potential for use within libraries for serving the patrons, for collaborating with colleagues, and as an outreaching means to patrons. For each of the sites reviewed, the reviewer gives a brief description of the site, indicates its strength and weakness and grades it as recommended or highly recommended for use by academic librarians. In addition, this paper provides the name and address of the reviewer of each site. The sites reviewed in the first part include Elluminate vRoom; Eventful; Facebook; Flickr; Freeconference; LinkedIn; Moodle; MySpace ; Ning; Second Life; Twitter ; Vyew; and Netvibes. The second part of this paper emphasizes the sites related to books, blogs, wikis, and Internet bookmarking. These sites include Blogger, WordPress, del.icio.us, Goodreads, Library Thing, Shelfari, Ma.gnolia, PBwiki, Wikispaces, Wikidot, TokBox, and Vox. All of these sites are accessible via http://sites.google.com/site/psqinternet/home

Cooper, J. D. (2008). Facebook applications for the library community. *Alabama Librarian,* 58(1), 8-11. This article's author, Cooper, says that the University of Montevallo moved into social networking after extensive work with technologies such as ListGarden RSS Feed Generator program to display the contents of the Library's popular browsing collection; Flicker for featuring photos taken by the library faculty, staff, and student workers; and Blogs to emphasize the availability of information when and where the user wanted it. He identifies Facebook applications as software programs that embed into profiles, allowing individuals and organizations to interact with their friends and contacts. From the perspective of the library practitioner, he says, these applications could be divided into two broad groups, those applications that are designed with libraries and librarians in mind, and those marketed to the general public that can be used by anyone to enhance their Web 2.0 presence. This article introduces applications from both groups, and discusses some of the ways that librarians at the University of Montevallo (UM) use these applications to connect with their patrons who use Facebook.

Crag, E. (2010). Use of social media in the member libraries of the business librarians association, *SCONUL Focus* (49), 12-14. This article describes the results of a biannual survey conducted by the Business Librarians Association (BLA) of UK in 2009 in order to identify the current state of the use of social media by academic business librarians and the services offered in their libraries. This article focuses on the use of social media by business librarians specifically on Twitter, Facebook, and blogs, the main question being whether these tools are used personally or professionally. Although no direct questions were posed to the librarians in the survey on the use of social media, it appears that many respondents used the comments fields to describe how their libraries were using social media. This article provides an overview of the methodology and key findings of the survey. The survey indicates that Facebook was the main social networking site used. Other most used tools used include YouTube for multimedia sharing, Delicious for social book marking, Twitter for micro-blogging, Meebo for instant messaging, and Netvibes to create start pages. It appears the students preferred the library to maintain a presence on social networking sites such as Facebook, because this provides a quick access point to library resources.

Dickson, A., & Holley, R. P. (2010). Social networking in academic libraries: The possibilities and the concerns. *New Library World,* 111(11-12), 468-479. With a view to finding the usage of social networking tools in academic libraries in the United States, this paper reviews articles and books published during 2006-2009 by searching the Library Literature and Information full text databases. The first author examines blogs and library accounts in various social networking sites. They examine other databases as well as the articles found in the bibliography of each of the article. Most of the papers reviewed appear to be anecdotal with little statistical analysis. The paper discusses the usage of major social networking sites such as Facebook, MySpace, Blogs and Wikis. The authors are of the view that the usage of social networking as an additional academic library outreach phenomenon emerged from Web 2.0 tools adding to the existing outreach method for reaching faculty and in turn students. They recommend promotion of social networking by academic libraries to be an effective method of student outreach in academic libraries provided the libraries take care to respect student privacy and provide equal coverage for all subject areas by avoiding potential negative consequences.

Draper, L., & Turnage, M. (2008). Blogmania: Blog use in academic libraries. *Internet Reference Services Quarterly,* 13(1), 15-55. Based on a review of literature, this article affirms that blogs can serve as a powerful medium for academic libraries to interact with students and faculty, to receive feedback from them, and to market library and information services effectively. With a view to ascertaining the extent of use of blogs for marketing of library services, the authors of this article conduct a survey via several list-serves. They analyze, summarize and present the responses from librarians on questions about the intended audience, statistics, and concerns on marketing of blogs. They conclude that academic libraries use blogs, some with greater success. They notice that popular blogs display recurrent themes such as news and events, marketing the library, and internal communication. They observe that most of the successful bloggers who responded were using multiple marketing strategies. The survey also demonstrates that librarians who post daily to the blog will receive more responses from users. The authors state that faculty support and a community culture is crucial for the success of blogs or any service, more so in the case of distance education students.

Emery, J. (2008). All we do is chat chat: Social networking for the electronic resources librarian. *Journal of Electronic Resources Librarianship,* 20(4), 205-209. Emery, the author of this paper, while acknowledging the popularity of social networking sites, presents a chorological account of sites starting with WELL (Whole Earth Lectronic Link) in 1985 followed by Classmates.com in 1995, Friendster in 2002, MySpace and LinkedIn in 2003, and Facbook in 2004. She mentions other sites including YouTube, LiveJournal, Tumblr, Twitter, and

Dopplr, which provide a basis of social networking via blogging in some cases and multi-tool access in other cases. This paper focuses mainly on describing advantages to the organization and in turn to the electronic resources librarian or information specialist to further the goals and objectives of their organization as well as to help in advancing their career. Their participation in social networks provides the organization with an informal network of other librarians or specialists who can be consulted when working on various projects and implementing new tools and services in a more timely fashion through Twitter or through Facebook. The biggest advantage of social networking for the individual librarian is instantaneously creating a network of colleagues with whom to consult and exchange ideas for furthering their career as well.

Farkas, M. (2009). Governing social media: Protect your library's brand online. *American Libraries,* 40(12), 35-35. Meredith Farkas, the author of this short article, says that social media sites such as blogs, Twitter, Facebook, and FriendFeed are used to connect with friends, family, and people around the world with common interests. In the process, she says that the boundary lines between private and public postings are being blurred. This blurring online of the divisions between professional and personal can affect an organization's reputation. She cites some cases where employees' use of social media has gotten themselves and their companies in trouble. The author wishes that all organizations could help their employees by framing policy guidelines identifying what kinds of information can and cannot be shared in online spaces. The author concludes by directing readers to an online database http://www.socialmediagovernance.com/policies.php. This online database presents policy guidelines with online access of several organizations such as industries, libraries, government or non-profit organizations, business products and service, healthcare organizations, and advertising agencies. In addition, this database includes a template for framing policy guidelines.

Farrell, A. M., Mayer, S. H., & Rethlefsen, M. L. (2011). Teaching web 2.0 beyond the library: Adventures in social media, the class. *Medical Reference Services Quarterly,* 30(3), 233-244. This is a very informative and detailed description of the introduction, teaching, and adoption of social media tools in a large, multidisciplinary group practice academic medical center with campuses in Arizona, Florida, Minnesota, Wisconsin, and Iowa. Eighteen libraries spread across all campuses make up the library system. The authors of this paper, who are librarians at the medical center, developed a customized Web 2.0 course for library staff, health science faculty, and nurse educators numbering over 50,000 individuals. The authors say that they developed a single, self-paced eight-module, blog-based course for all employees in cooperation and coordination with the public affairs department. The modules included blogging, RSS, wikis, online collaboration tools, social bookmarking, OPACs, podcasts, mash-ups, and social media. The instructors did not put screen cast tutorials on YouTube, as it was felt the content on YouTube could prove harmful to the institution's reputation. The program, which spanned a 13-week period, provided employees with the opportunity receive credit on their employee transcript upon completion at each module and the passing of a brief assessment. The authors opine that even though a high number of learners accessed the course, the completion percentage was low since there was no requirement to complete the course.

Ferguson, C. (2007). Technology left behind -- making friends online: Library use of social networking services. *Against the Grain,* 19(3), 86-87. Ferguson, the author of this article, citing other authors, highlights various ways in which people are using social media for networking with friends, colleagues, and customers. He says that social networking Web sites bring together under one umbrella a variety of relationship management tools in an easy-to-use, free interface, allowing users a variety of methods for keeping in touch with one another. He looks at social networking sites MySpace and Facebook, and mentions how libraries are using these sites to connect with patrons and each other. He points out both these sites serve one and the same purpose, the main difference being which audience they serve. Facebook shares many similarities with MySpace but its users remain college-age students, making it an ideal interface for college and university libraries looking to connect with their patrons. The author says that the MySpace interface provides a number of networking tools in a relatively self-explanatory interface, including facilities that enable users to send messages back and forth to each other, to blog, and post bulletins to friends, to leave comments for other MySpace users, and to instant message.

Fernandez, J. (2009).A SWOT analysis for social media in libraries. *Online (Weston, Conn.),* 33(5), 35-37. This article is a lucid discussion of the importance of conducting a SWOT (Strengths, Weaknesses, Opportunities, and Threats) analysis of social networking tools in libraries to justify their use in library management. The author presents a generalized SWOT analysis. The Strengths that were identified include free availability, ease of instant set, ability to reach out to patrons at shortest time, facility of users to contribute their own ideas, possibility of librarians to think outside the box, and the capability of site administrators to exercise some control over the content and users' interaction with librarians. The weaknesses mentioned include limitations on the amount of information one can input, potential exposure of libraries to criticism, downloading problems with some organizations, limitations imposed by blogs in the choice of website design, and the limits to the number of characters as in Twitter. Opportunities include marketing of services and collections to library clientele, the facility to reach a wide range of users and attract new users, and the opportunity to hear from patrons about the kind of services they want. Also present is the capability of using a variety of means in reaching audience of online users who are considered Digital Natives as well as those who are deemed to be Digital Immigrants. Threats include potential sabotage of social websites in many ways as they are beyond the control of the librarians, ease of unsubscribing at the click of a button, and the possibility of big threat media providers folding up at any time, causing loss to libraries in many ways.

Fernandez, P. (2010). Privacy and generation Y: Applying library values to social networking sites. *Community & Junior College Libraries,* 16(2), 100-113. While there appears to be no common definition, Generation Y, also known as the millennial kids or Net Generation, refers to people born in the1980s and early the 1990s, and sometimes includes those born as late as the year 2000. The author, Fernandez, in this article infers from literature review, both the practical and the philosophical aspects of the value of privacy and the typical characteristics of generation Y students who are the primary clientele of undergraduate college libraries. He elaborates how the value of privacy affects libraries attempting to operate in a for-profit mediated space such as social networking sites. He conceptualizes five recommendations that could guide librarians while dealing with privacy issues in social networking sites where potential threats to privacy have expanded and confidentiality is no longer a clear concern. These recommendations emphasize the need for librarians to be translators and interpreters of transferred information through social networking sites, rather than relying on the information's value. Fernandez encourages librarians to take a leadership role in the public debate on privacy and asks them to respect patrons' boundaries. He stresses the need for constant update of institutional policies governing social media in order to set a model for privacy-conscious behavior in the realm of emerging technologies.

Fiehn, B. (2008). Social networking and your library OPAC! *MultiMedia & Internet@Schools,* 15(5), 27-29. This article discusses the need to incorporate social networking applications into online public access catalogs (OPACs) of school libraries. The author says that the enhancement of OPACs will be engaging for students and for teachers alike through which applications such as book reviews and recommendations, which would provide a way for teachers and students to communicate beyond the school setting and the school term. She acknowledges that several school media specialists and other educators are well acquainted with social networking tools such as MySpace, tagging sites such as Delicious and LibraryThing, wikis, and blogs. However, in her interaction with the media specialists, she notices hesitation based on lack of knowledge of how it would work in their schools and how much time it would take to monitor student input. Through the discussion, this paper presents several examples of vendors as well as schools that have incorporated and implemented social networking applications in their OPACs.

Fiehn, B. (2009). Social networking through your library automation system: What librarians and vendors have to say. *MultiMedia & Internet@Schools,* 16(5), 28-31. This article is based on the findings of a survey by Barbara Fiehn, author of this paper, of the use of social networking sites by school library media specialists in their school automation system. It also includes comments of interviews by vendors at the annual ALA conference in 2009 conducted by the author. She reasons that since school students are already using social networking applications outside of school, they should have an environment that is congenial and friendly within school automation systems. She observes that encouraging students to interact with the library staff and each other via the library catalog could bring students to the virtual library interface. She highlights social networking possibilities such as book reviewing, ratings, recommending purchases, sharing of book lists, and discussion groups. She recalls administrative concerns expressed by the media specialists in incorporating social network tools in the school automation system. The article presents salient features of various vendors interviewed that could facilitate the school systems in adopting social networking sites.

Fitzpatrick, M. (2006). At issue: Should congress require schools and public libraries to block social-networking web sites? Yes. *CQ Researcher,* 16(27), 641. This article centers round the bill introduced in 2006 by Rep. Michael Fitzpatrick in the U.S. House of Representatives that aimed to restrict social networking Web sites as well as pornography sites in schools and libraries, and chat rooms. The article summarizes views of various members advanced for and against the bill. The main reason expressed for blocking the sites is that for children the social networks open the door to many dangers, including online bullying and exposure to child predators, as supervision currently is completely inadequate. However, critics of the bill say that blocking access is nearly impossible without inadvertently blocking valuable portions of the Internet. They say that by blocking sites such as MySpace and Facebook, would also block many other sites including blogging tools, mailing lists, video and pod-cast sites, photo-sharing sites and educational sites like NeoPets, where kids create virtual pets and participate in educational games. The legislation could also affect distance-learning programs. Furthermore, the critics feel it unwise to keep teachers and librarians away from social-networking technology who can utilize the technology constructively and safely. Another argument against restricting access is that children in wealthier families could still access school-blocked InteRethlefsenRrnet sites from home, while students without Internet are put to disadvantage.

Fletcher, J. (2010). Social networking fires up academic librarians. *Multimedia Information and Technology,* 36(4), 20-21. This is an anecdotal summary of the experiences shared by academic librarians in a meeting at Liverpool John Moores University, UK, on the use of social networking sites in their own institutions. The author says that they had an interesting and timely microcosmic look at what academic libraries are doing in the realm of social networking while using Facebook, Twitter, wikis, Prezi, Flickr, Google Analytics, Foursquare, GoWalla, and library blogs.

Ganster, L., & Schumacher, B. (2009).Expanding beyond our library walls: Building an active online community through Facebook. *Journal of Web Librarianship,* 3(2), 111-128. The authors of this article demonstrate how Facebook can be used in academic libraries to develop an outreach presence for marketing of library services as well as for communicating information online with the patrons. Unlike much of the literature examined by the authors, this article focuses on the use of Facebook's newest feature: customizable Facebook Pages. The authors explore the use of Facebook Pages to virtually reach out to patrons and market library services. Based on user response and Page statistics, the authors observe that the use of Facebook Pages provided a welcome extension of services and a unique form of outreach that could reach beyond the campus community to the commuting patrons. The authors mention that by having a Facebook page on the homepage of the institution, librarians can update and inform students, faculty, and staff of new events, workshops, library services, and resources. The article mentions that through blogs and RSS, the fans of the library can provide discussion and feedback regarding library services. They further explain the design process, including the use of third-party and custom applications. The authors mention that they maintain an active online community that reaches more than 300 fans. Fans provide discussion and feedback regarding library services, offering a more interactive extension of the Libraries homepage.

Gauder, B. (2007). Social networking encourages teen library usage at Denver public. *NextSpace,* (7), 12-13. This article says that based on a survey that reported MySpace as the favorite online site of teenagers; the Denver (Colorado) Public Library developed a social networking site in 2006. The author states that the site offers abundant links to online activities that teens use to stay connected. The links to library resources aimed at the teen age group include homework help and 24/7 online reference and materials for checkout. The article says that another link on Denver Public Library's teen site provides resources for further exploration, including many social networking tools. The author says that since the launch of the MySpace page, Denver Public Library has developed a number of activities aimed at keeping the library a teen-friendly place such as a YouTube video contest, a bookmark contest for its summer reading program, and invitations to write online reviews for books, movies and CDs in the library's collection. The author says that by going to where the teens are the library can give them a new idea of what a library is and make them feel comfortable in the library, thereby increasing the traffic to the library.

Gordon, R. S., & Stephens, M. (2007). Tech Tips for Every Librarian - Building a Community: Create Your Own Social Network .*Computers in Libraries,* 27 (10), 46. This article discusses various freely available social network tools for libraries for creating social network sites. These resources include Ning, Facebook, Flickr, FreeForums, Indiana Librarians Prototype, Wikipedia, and WordPress. The authors state that staff can use Facebook Group for library wide polls, program planning and general discussion. They can provide feeds from the library's blogs into the Group as well. Ning, a social networking service similar to Facebook, has the ability to create groups, discussion forums, integrated blogs, tag clouds and integrated video and photos. Users can customize their personal pages too. Guidelines for promoting social networking sites are presented. The paper lists the URLs of the above mentioned applications (Adapted from source).

Griffey, J. (2010).Social networking and the library. *Library Technology Reports*, 46(8), 34-37. This article focuses on social networking sites vis-à-vis privacy and freedom of information in libraries. The author observes that the rise of online social networks and their connectivity in recent times has resulted in the decline of privacy. For example, the author says that when patrons checked out library material, it was easy for libraries to protect their identity and privacy. But when they use social networking sites on library computers in library networks, it becomes difficult to manage patron's identity as well as the library network with several layers of networks. In such cases the patron's identity gets unintentionally disclosed to social network sites. Therefore, the author says, libraries have attempted interacting with patrons within the various sites, and providing access and sometimes user training on how best to use sites like Facebook, Twitter, FriendFeed, and more. The paper discusses two conflicting points, assisting in access to networks that potentially affect privacy and protecting information about the patrons.

Harris, A., & Lesick, S. (2007). Libraries get personal: Facebook applications, Google gadgets, and MySpace profiles. *Library Hi Tech News,* 24(8), 30-32. This is a general article describing applications, gadgets, and profiles that libraries have developed and distributed via Facebook, iGoogle, and MySpace communities. The authors say that an increasing number of libraries and library-related organizations are creating practical tools using Web 2.0 technologies complementing previous methods employed by libraries, guiding the patrons through the library experience without forcing them to leave the familiarity of their favorite sites. The paper describes the use of specific tools with examples from various libraries. The authors explain how the library related application of Facebook is used for displaying RSS feeds, searching an outside resource, and cataloging a person's recently seen movies. They describe how, with MySpace, organizations can have their own profile page linking key resources such as article databases and reference guides on the profile page to serve as a different homepage. They mention the use of MySpace blogs to keep their patrons up-to-date on library events. They illustrate how Google gadgets are used through iGoogle for RSS feed to readers, search boxes for non-Google resources, weather forecasts, calendars, and games.

Hendrix, D., Chiarella, D., Hasman, L., & Murphy, S. (2009). Use of Facebook in academic health sciences libraries. *Journal of the Medical Library Association,* 97(1), 43-46. The authors recognize the benefits of Facebook in health libraries with dispersed users. From literature they reviewed, they notice lack of research-based studies on the use of Facebook in health libraries. With a view to find the extent and nature of Facebook use and the perceived success of institutional Facebook pages, the authors conduct a study of the views of heads of the reference services, public services, outreach librarians, and library directors of the member libraries of the

Association of Academic Health Sciences Libraries. Based on the analysis of the data that maintain Facebook pages and libraries that do not maintain Facebook pages, the paper concludes that Facebook use by health sciences academic libraries is still at an evolving stage. It says that most libraries use Facebook for library promotional purposes such as for announcements, posting of photos, chat reference, and as a mark of presence in the social network. The majority of libraries using it do not have a strong opinion on the current or future success of their libraries' Facebook presence.

Infield, N. (2009). Engaging with social media in the Business & Intellectual Property Centre (BIPC) at the British Library: News from the National. *Business Information Review,* 26(1), 57-58. This article describes the efforts of Business & Intellectual Property Centre (BIPC) of British Library, U K, in marketing their services and reaching its diverse audience consisting of inventors, aspiring entrepreneurs, social entrepreneurs, small business owners, and students. Not satisfied with conventional channels, the author says, that they started experimenting in reaching their patrons through social media tools such as Blogs, Twitter, Facebook, MySpace, Bebo, and YouTube. The channel YouTube enables BIPC to collect all of the videos in one place and monitor their usage. He finds Facebook as the preferred choice of graduates and professionals, with MySpace and Bebo the predominantly preferred choice of music fans. He says that the adoption of social networking tools has proved to be successful as evidenced by a manifold increase in page views as well as faster growth in membership numbers for British Library Entrepreneur and SME Network (Facebook, BIPC). The author concludes in saying that although they experimented with various tools, finally they preferred Facebook over MySpace and Bebo.

Jacobson, T. B. (2011). Facebook as a library tool: Perceived vs. actual use. *College & Research Libraries,* 72(1), 79-90. The author of this paper, Jacobson, categorizes published literature on Facebook into five broad types, namely: 'how to based' studies, survey based studies, library-centered case studies, service-provided analysis, and perceived-use studies. Noticing very few studies on perceived use studies, he focuses on reported versus actual use of Facebook in libraries to identify discrepancies between perceived goals and actual use. The author uses the data of a study by Hendrix and others on the use of Facebook in libraries as a guide to gauge the perceived and actual uses for Facebook and compares it with the data he gathered. The Hendrix study focused Facebook use on announcements/marketing, photos, reference services; forums for users; RSVP to events, OPAC search, database search; employee announcements, and employee communication. From the analysis, the author finds noticeable differences in the perceived and actual rankings qualitatively. He finds in Facebook a better tool for libraries that host a lot of events, exhibits, workshops, and other activities, as its top use is for announcements and marketing.

Jenkins, H. (2006). At issue: Should congress require schools and public libraries to block social-networking web sites? no. *CQ Researcher,* 16(27), 641. This article presents the discussion on The Deleting Online Predators Act of 2006 (DOPA), a bill brought before the United States House of Representatives on May 9, 2006 by Republican Pennsylvania Representative (R-PA) Mike Fitzpatrick. The bill, if enacted, would require public schools and libraries to bar access to social-networking sites and chat rooms as well as to pornography sites. The bill's proponents argue that restrictions on access to social networking websites are necessary to protect children from online predators, whether the predators are sexually oriented offenders or even simple online bullies. The arguments against the bill focus on efforts to revise it to address the problem of online predators, while at the same time preventing the blocking of harmless and/or educational websites. They say that this bill will not delete online predators. On the other hand, it will delete legitimate Web content from schools and libraries. They point out that because technology plays a major role in the business world, it is unwise to deprive students of it in schools and libraries. One representative of an educational institute opposes the bill because teachers are using social networking technology to create blogs for knowledge sharing in schools and to communicate expectations about homework with students and parents.

Jennings, S., & Price, J. (2008). "Be my friend" using Facebook in libraries. *Tennessee Libraries,* 58(2), 1-3. This article presents general discussions on the role of Facbook in libraries and its applications. The authors describe Facebook as a powerful tool for libraries to connect with users and deliver services from a distance. They provide a history of Facebook, its potential uses for librarians, key privacy issues and possible legal issues surrounding the use of social networking site for communication. The presenters discuss four areas regarding the use of Facebook in libraries: Personal accounts for librarians; useful applications for libraries; library event publicity; and, joining and creating "groups." The authors say that by creating a Facebook account, the librarian creates a virtual "office" where users can contact them. This creates visibility for the librarian and a space for Reader's Advisory. Further, they say that Facebook offers better personalized service for the patrons, and an additional and "safe" avenue for those that might have communication or social challenges. Upon perusing this article, one finds many Facebook applications.

Kho, N. D. (2011). Social media in libraries: Keys to deeper engagement. *Information Today,* 28(6), 1, 31-2. Quoting from the writings of several authors, the author of this paper presents a suggestive view for librarians in successfully adopting social media in their libraries. He finds differences in usage numbers in one and the same library from site to site such as Facebook, Twitter, and YouTube. He points out that libraries can benefit from social media by reaching a broader audience, building relationships with customers, communicating with patrons, marketing their resources and services, and most importantly setting a goal supported by management, displaying a readiness to try or reject new things. He says that librarians also need to embrace prioritization and content management tools, incorporating location-based technology into their work. He prefers experimentation, but not investing time and money where it is not working. He says the question is not about finding the time to do social media, but it is about figuring out what you need to stop doing in its place.

King, D. L. (2011). Facebook for libraries. *American Libraries,* 42(5), 42-45.This author, King, narrates his personal experiences on Facebook and says it is the most popular social networking site to stay in contact with the community and an easy to use tool. He mentions statistics from various polls and studies and says that about 41 percent of the U.S. population has a personal Facebook profile and half of these users log on to their accounts every day.He mentions that several of his professional colleagues and most of his family have Facebook accounts. He urges all librarians to create a Facebook account for their libraries, for which there is no monetary charge. The author asks new Facebook users to figure out first a couple of practical things such as who will do the Page, answer questions, post events, post updates, keep track of user names, and passwords. Also, he asks them to create some one-year goals for the Facebook presence such as number of status updates to post per day/ week or the number of fans needed, in addition to types of content planned for the specific audience to be focused. The author hopes that when the Facebook community gets the content they want, they would spontaneously become library Facebook fans.

Kniffel, L. (2008). Medical librarians get healthy dose of social networking. American Libraries, 39(7),32.This is a news item reporting on the opening remarks given by Medical Library Association President Mark Funk on the theme " communication, community, openness, participation, and connecting" presented at the of MLA 2.0 at Chicago conference. He observes that bureaucrats are becoming less hierarchical and resorting to Web 2.0 tools such as blogs, wikis, RSS feeds, and podcasts. This article includes comments by other speakers.

Kranich, N. (2007). Librarians and teen privacy in the age of social networking. *Knowledge Quest,* 36(2), 34-37. This article, while discussing issues related to teenagers' attitude' to privacy, contends with the notion that teenagers are not careful in disclosing their personal information while posting online. Citing a study by the Pew Internet and American Life Project, the author says that the majority 55percent of teens who place their personal profiles online take steps to protect themselves from areas of risk. She says that teens are well aware of the risks they face when they present themselves online. This article mentions various laws and rules governing privacy issues in federal and state constitutions and says that because of piecemeal approach to privacy policy, access to and protection of consumer records varies widely from one type of service to another and from state to state. She says that the narrative in the news media amplifies the dangers for teens of exposing too much personal information to criminal or commercial predators by overlooking the extraordinary benefits of social networking. This paper encourages librarians to observe the guidelines documented by ALAs Young Adult Library Services.

Krishnamurthy, M., & Ashwath, L. (2010). Social network technology and its implications for libraries: Transforming the library services through the web. *SRELS Journal of Information Management,* 47(3), 283-288. This is a theoretical paper highlighting the salient features of social networking sites in general in relation to library services. The authors mention that social networking websites offer a social media platform free of charge for users who share the content online. They are of the view that while Web 2.0 tools and services are meant to foster new modes of connectivity, collaboration, information sharing, and content development, the term Library 2.0refers to providing focus on how libraries can make their services visible to society and end users. The paper says that although informal social networking sites emerged since the inception of the Web, dedicated social networking sites cropped up only since 2003. The authors discuss various issues in social networks such as structure of social networks, social software applications, social software in libraries, and challenges and issues that have an impact upon the provision of social networks. They notice increasing interest in libraries and librarians in exploring social networking sites for both personal and professional resources.

Kroski, E. (2007). The social tools of web 2.0: Opportunities for academic libraries. *Choice,* 44(12), 2011-2021. This article outlines the role of the Web which has led to a new breed of software applications capable of accomplishing sophisticated tasks with little technical know-how. The emergence of social tools has empowered ordinary people to connect and participate in a global conversation by linking people to people as well as to information. The author explores the Web 2.0 social tools and their potential uses within academic libraries. He broadly categorizes the social tools and discusses them in four main sections: content collaboration (wikis and online office applications), social bookmarking, media sharing, and social networking. For each type of social tool, the category is first described with examples in relation to potential and actual use in academic libraries. Tools and sites indicated in the text in italics are listed alphabetically within the four main sections of the Links Cited list following the conclusion of the essay.

Kroski, E. (2009). Should your library have a social media policy? *School Library Journal*, 55(10), 44-46. This article acknowledges the exorbitant growth in the percentage of users making their presence on social networking sites and says that the distinction between private and public purposes of postings is fading as seemingly everyone has a Facebook or Twitter profile on social media. The author says that the policy is a useful way for setting some ground rules regarding social media for staff and users with regard to their online activities. He says that it would also serve as a reminder that the content that they post is not private and may ultimately reflect on the organization. The author outlines what an individual policy should include concerning social media as a whole or by addressing different types of applications such as blogs, Facebook, and other social networks, and micro-blogging services like Twitter. The paper suggests some specific points for the employees to follow while posting their comments. The points include disclaimers on the personal blog and other social sites stating opinions are not those of employers; respect for copyright; respect to colleagues; avoidance of online fights or inflammatory arguments; the posting accurate information, and consultation of the employee manual.

Lancaster, N. (2008). Web 2.0 -- hype or helpful? *Public Library Journal,* 23(3), 6-8. The author, Nigel Lancaster, discusses how Web 2.0 and social networking tools can promote libraries and their resources to a wider audience. He says that Web 2.0 and social networking have been increasingly getting popular in the technology world since the term was coined 2004. He recognizes seven Web 2.0 categories: blogs, mashups, podcasting, RSS, social networking, widgets, and wikis, and states that all of these tools could be included in the communication channels of public libraries. The author says that libraries can improve communications with users by using Web 2.0 to foster and create new citizen interfaces, discussion groups and online activities, along the lines of mainstream social networking sites such as Facebook and MySpace. The article says that related resources could be integrated into the OPAC search, in the form of automatic searching of local authority and national websites, and paid-for services and reader development services such as book reviews and suggestions that could be included as part of the library's online presence. Local information or 'community-owned information', such as materials from archives, clubs and societies, record offices and picture libraries, could appear on the site in addition to provision in leaflet form. The author encourages library chiefs to adopt new technology if they are to make the most of the opportunities offered by Web 2.0 tools.

Landau, R. (2010). Solo librarian and outreach to hospital staff using web 2.0 technologies. *Medical Reference Services Quarterly,* 29 (1), 75-84. This is a case study of experimentation and implementation of two social media tools, Delicious and Bloglines, in a 330-bed hospital setting. The author narrates her experiences about how after gaining training in an online course on Web 2.0 technologies; she has implemented these two technologies by creating accounts. She describes the features of the tool, Delicious, and says that instead of bookmarking favorite sites on one's own computer, they can be saved to sit on an Internet site so that users can retrieve from any computer online. She says that another feature, tagging favorite sites, permits multiple subject headings (tags) for a link and gives users more than one way to find a resource. She says that both technologies, Delicious and Blogline, are advantageous to librarians and library users as they require a minimum of time to maintain and they expand library services outside the confines of the physical library and hospital.

Landis, C. (2007).Connecting to Users with Facebook. *Georgia Library Quarterly*, 43(4), 6. The author acknowledges the popularity of social networking with a wide variety of library users and considers that the sites MySpace and Facebook are the highest ranked sites for Web traffic. He says that these sites appeal to users because they provide a variety of services in one interface and users are able to create a profile, make connections with people they know (called "friending"), send messages, and join groups, share photos, and comment on friends' profiles. A reference librarian at Valdosta State University library, he uses Facebook to keep up with friends from college and his Master of Library and Information Science (MLIS) program. He decided to set up an "Ask a Librarian" group for students at the university. This group in Facebook allows the students to get help at their point of need in a user interface with which that they are already familiar. In addition, the group message board retains questions and answers, allowing students to find answers to common questions. The author says that although he tried advertising the group via flyers around campus, he found that most of the students joined by word of mouth--either they were in a library instruction session where he mentioned the group, or they had heard about it from friends (Adapted from source).

Larson, M., & Chats, H. (2010).The relevancy of twitter to patron usage and workflow processes in libraries. *ELearn,* 2010 (10), 7. This is a summary of the relevance of twitter and its usage in academic libraries. Citing several other authors, the authors of this article say that the adoption of Twitter will benefit academic libraries in several ways such as creating functional environments in classrooms, and workplaces changing workflow process, as well as serving as a teaching and research tool. They say that Twitter has the potential to be used for micro blogging as a broadcast medium, as a reference tool, as a search engine, and as a manager of third-party information. Quoting another author they say that it can be used for making a personal connection with other librarians by sharing their favorite new book, video of the day, quote of the day, or blog post; and for scheduling to meet fellow librarians at a conference, or organize a professional tweet-up in your area. Yet another author says that Twitter allows the library academic staff to interact with their library technology colleagues as an instant feedback tool with instant feedback. Finally, they say that the utilization of Twitter in libraries by librarians is important because it allows them to make connections.

Laskaris, R. (2008)."I don't even know this person!": Academic libraries on Facebook. *Access (1204-0472),* 14(2), 21-23. This is a narration of a reference librarian in a science and engineering library who was assigned to investigate Facebook groups and to create a group for his library. The author says that in order to find what other libraries are doing, he surveys over 200 Facebook groups of various academic organizations created by librarians and finds that some groups were created to reach out to students and some to interact with the coworkers in the library. He states that the membership was very low some, in single digits. With regard to the content, he finds that some were posting in general, most of groups featured photos and contact information of their respective libraries. Librarians posted messages on the Wall, invited students to contribute suggestions and comments, made general announcements, and initiated discussion topics. He says that most groups were dead. He concludes that a library's presence on Facebook as a group seemed to be valuable more as a public relations device than as a practical means of service delivery. He suggests that for Facebook to be valuable to students, it should have an application that integrates with library systems to provide access from Facebook into the OPAC, patron accounts etc.

Libraries and social networking: The thoughts of nine experts about our increasingly online lives. (2007). *NextSpace,* (7), 4-10. This article presents the thoughts of nine experts about online lives with special reference to social networking. In summary, they say that although the term social networking is new, the concepts behind it - sharing content, collaborating with others, and creating community - have been around for a long time. What is new is the digital medium, which makes connecting with other people faster, easier and more accessible to a wider population than it is ever has been before. They opine that social networking has been around for a long time, as early as the time of Plato in 400 B.C., when scholars and philosophers studied and analyzed the formation and interaction of groups of people. In their view, the challenge is how to apply social networking in a digital age to enhance and extend the public service mission of libraries, museums and archives. The experts analyze the role of various social networking sites and delineate the fields where these sites are applicable. The article is very informative and worth noting.

Library to archive groundbreaking social network. (2010).*Library of Congress Information Bulletin,* 69(5), 84-86. This is a news item reporting the announcement by the Communications Director of the Library of Congress about archiving of ALL public tweets gifted by Twitter. It says that Twitter processes more than 50 million tweets per day from people around the world. The Library will receive all public tweets--which number in the billions--from the 2006 inception of the service to the present. The article quotes the Librarian of the Library of Congress and says that the Twitter digital archives have the potential for research into the contemporary way of life and will provide detailed evidence about how the technology-based social networks form evolved over time. This Twitter archive will be a valuable research tool providing access for very large sets of born-digital materials. The article quotes other speakers who state that Twitter archive will be one of the most informative resources available on modern-day culture, including economic, social and political trends, as well as consumer behavior and social trends. This article lists the URL of President Obama's tweet about winning the election, and other worthwhile URLs.

Lindsay, E. B. (2009).Using social networking in the library. *Public Services Quarterly,* 5(3), 208-211. The author of this paper while acknowledging the popularity of various social networking tools such as Twitter, Facebook, Second Life, highlights some of the early research that has been done and recommends a few papers by various authors on Web 2.0 technologies. She summarizes the papers along with bibliographic information for the guidance of librarians. The articles mentioned in this paper focus on wide ranging issues, such as Facebook, MySpace, and student outreach; Library 2.0 and the consumer as producer; Facebook adoption in an academic library; Facebook as a communication mechanism; Ethics from Web 1.0 to Web 2.0; Use of the Internet in school libraries and media centers; Lessons learnt from Second Life; and Use of Twitter outreach efforts for outreaching purpose.

Maness, J. M. (2006). Library 2.0 theory: Web 2.0 and its implications for libraries, *Webology,* 3(2). This author offers a definition for "Library 2.0" and puts forward a theory for "Library 2.0". Says that changing Web as "Web 2.0" will have substantial implications for libraries calling for a new paradigm for librarianship. He applies this theory and definition addressing how Web 2.0 technologies can bring in changes in libraries in providing access to their collections and user support for that access. He advances the theory for Library 2.0 and says that it could have four essential elements: user-centered; socially rich; communally innovative; and provide a multi-media experience. He describes social networking as the most promising and embracing technology enabling messaging, blogging, streaming media, and tagging. He comments on popular sites such as MySpace, Facbook, Delicious, Frapper, and Flickr. He describes other noteworthy tool LibraryThing and says it enables users to catalog their books and view what other users share those books. He concludes by observing that social networks, in some sense, as Library 2.0 and says that the face of the library's web-presence in future might look very much like a social network interface.

Mathews, B. S. (2007).Libraries' place in virtual social networks. *Journal of Web Librarianship,* 1(2), 71-74. This paper asks librarians to consider their role in the virtual world of social networking and says that the new premise is that they can no longer sit back and wait for patrons to approach them. He encourages librarians to provide library services to patrons wherever they are by repackaging the content into a ready-to-share format. He asks for the use of social networking tools such as MySpace to advertise library identity, and encourages librarian to open the channels of conversation and enter into a public dialogue with users by collecting their experiences, feedback, and recommendations and sharing them openly. The author suggests that the library should post photos of users playing games, working collaboratively on assignments, or rehearsing a presentation, emphasizing the flexibility of the space. He encourages the librarians to socialize successfully with personalized comments focusing on solving problems by understanding the culture and providing giveaways, exclusive content, or other enticements to give users a reason to come back. Since Facebook is deleting all library profiles from their network, stating that the accounts are for individuals, and prohibits messages with advertising or promotional content, the author feels the library is the best place to promote library services.

McDermott, I. E. (2007). All a-twitter about web 2.0: What does it offer libraries? *Searcher,* 15(9). This author says that with the advent of web.2 .0 tools, librarians have become heavily dependent on it even for several jobs in their day to day library work, more particularly reference service. The term Web.2.0, he says, encompasses Websites that host or allow the production of user-generated Web content, as well as of social networking. He observes that over the years, several useful Web 2.0 applications have emerged making information professionals' job quite easy. Based on a blog 'Communication Over tones', the author divides web 2.0 or social media tools into seven major categories: Publishing platforms, such as blogs and podcasts; social networking sites, such as MySpace and Facebook; democratized content networks, such as Digg and Wikipedia that allow users to add, change, or rate content; virtual networking platforms, such as Second Life ; information aggregators, such as Memorandum, which automatically collect headlines on a single general topic from a collection of sources; edited social news platforms sites, such as Spin Thicket, that post news stories referred by users; and content distribution sites that allow users to create or collect and distribute content, such as del.icio.us or Scrapblog . The paper provides a sampling of some Web 2.0 services that some libraries have found useful. However, the author says that not all these types of sites will serve the library as an organization.

McKenna, B. (2011). U.K. University libraries and social media. *Information Today,* 28(2), 14-15. The author of this column, while acknowledging how European STM publishers are using social media as a part of their marketing strategies in reaching out to customers, looks at the trends in some universes in the UK in marketing their special collections. He says that the University of Glasgow (Scotland) library, as an active social media user, with its blog posts promotes special collections such as The Hunterian Psalter, and primary source materials at Victorian Music Hall and Glasgow's unofficial anthem, "Glasgow Belongs to Me". He cites the university's Facebook page, a Library on Demand section (videos hosted via YouTube), and 2,462 images primarily from its special collections section on Flickr. He mentions that the University of Oxford's libraries direct their users to a social media directory at Bodleian Libraries at www.bodleian.ox.ac.uk/libraries/libraries/web2. The article also mentions Warwick University Library and Taylor Institution Library. The author observes that many University of Oxford libraries now communicate with their users through a variety of social media such as blogs, Facebook and Twitter.

Miller, S., & Jensen, L. A. (2007). Connecting and Communicating with Students on Facebook (cover story). *Computers in Libraries*, 27(8), 18-22. This is a very useful article giving practical tips to librarians in promoting library Facebook pages. The authors point out that students visit Facebook for connection and not for reading library material, as most of them read information that Facebook puts in front of them, not what they seek out on their own. They urge librarians to connect with patrons before effectively promoting the services to them. They recommend several ways of connecting the library's Facebook such as connecting all of the student workers at the library, which will be more visible to students and friends and their Friends; connecting librarians' instructional sessions and asking all of the students in them to be a Friend; displaying the profile during instructional sessions; and friending new students at semester welcome. The authors observe that students join a multitude of Groups but do very little to participate in any of them. The most powerful aspect of promotion of a Facebook profile appears to be friending and feeding, continuous postings. The article concludes by saying 'Without Friends, Facebook is a cold, lonely world.'

Milstein, S. (2009). Twitter FOR libraries (and librarians). *Computers in Libraries,* 29(5), 17-18. This is an introductory article briefly describing the what, why, and how of Twitter, a free and fast growing messaging service. The author says that Twitter helps to send and receive short messages limited to 140 characters, called Tweets via the web or via SMS using a mobile phone. This medium is also known as "microblogging." Like full-sized blogging, the pint-sized version is useful for exchanging many different kinds of information. This article says that a library could share news that patrons want such as about readings, lectures, and book sales; newly available resources; or changes in the building hours, interesting news stories about literacy or about libraries. This paper gives a sampling of various libraries in the U.S. and the purpose for which the Twitter is used. They include Public libraries, university libraries, and special libraries. The article provides tips to use Twitter effectively.

Morris, D. (2010). Leeds met library Facebook application. *SCONUL Focus,* (48), 23-25. The article offers information on the Facebook Inc. application for the library of the Leeds Metropolitan (Leeds Met) University. It states that the Facebook application was intended for sending a library catalogue search box to a profile in Facebook, with delivery of customized user data that include details of the library record. It also mentions that the application was planned to offer links to the online self-service functions and library website. It adds that after the application's launch, there have been 50-60 regular users every month and more than 250 total visitors.(Adapted from source).

Magolis, D. (2008).Connecting with online library research methods course students in Facebook. *Pennsylvania Library Association Bulletin,* 63(6), 8-10. This article describes how the author has adopted the social networking site Facebook, to communicate with students and provide web-based courses to them. The author narrates the process of orienting, integrating, and communicating with students, as well as ways to use Facebook as a means of student assessment. He finds in Facebook a better tool for grading when compared with Blackboard. He says that he has used Facebook group to post announcements, to send mass and individual messages, and to create a threaded discussion board. The author says that the students in the class were encouraged to provide feedback on the medium via a course survey. At the end of the semester he asks the students to participate in an anonymous online survey regarding their Web-based learning experiences. He summarizes the responses from the students and their communication and learning experiences.

Mullan, J. (2009). Should we be more social? Law librarians and social media. *Legal Information Management,* 9(3), 175-181. The author, a law librarian, examines how legal information specialists could use social networking tools for increasing productivity. He observes that employees with extensive personal online networks were more productive than their colleagues. He briefly describes the features of some sites useful to law librarians and illustrates them for what purpose they can be used. Twitter, he says, is perfect places for individuals to showcase their talents and highlight resources they think will be of interest to their Twitter followers; Facebook, a great way to communicate and share information with peers; LinkedIn, a significant way in which connections can help people build their profiles and reputations online. Ning enables users to create their own social networks around specific interests, with their own visual design; Delicious enables one to save any resources one finds on the internet; Slideshare helps to publish slides on the web, so that they can be found and shared by a wide audience; and Friendfeed "aggregates" an individual's activity from other social media sites and creates a feed or "stream" of information. He points out privacy and time as major concerns for one using a social media site.

Mumenthaler, R. (2010). Library promotion using Facebook advertising: Does it work? *International Leads,* 24(4), 5. The author of this article describes the use of the social network site, Facebook, as a marketing tool for promoting library services and the problems encountered while doing so. He says that the ETH-Bibliothek of the Swiss Institute of Technology created a Facebook page, connected the page with the library homepage, and further connected it with other social media such as Twitter and blogs, and invited personal friends to become fans. He says that the campaign has resulted in the increase of number of Facebook fans. However, the author says that the connection between the personal Facebook accounts of the administrator with the institutional page has landed in problems. He says that a survey on the use of Facebook in the library found most people not paying attention to promotional materials in social networks. As such, the author says that the library has discontinued the promotional campaign and removed the ads from Facebook. He says that using Facebook ads is an interesting, but not successful, experience.

Nicholas, D., Watkinson, A., Rowlands, I., & Jubb, M. (2011). Social media, academic research and the role of university libraries. *The Journal of Academic Librarianship*, 373-375. This article focuses on the findings of deliberations of the CIBER research group researching the use of social media for research by academics. It says that social media is impacting significantly the scholarly communication and research process. As a corollary, the group felt that if the social media is impacting on the academic researcher, then it must be impacting on university libraries too. Contrary to this assumption, the findings say that in the emerging social media environment, libraries are very much an afterthought. The findings reveal that libraries do not have a strong and visible presence in the existing digital scholarly space and therefore are not the natural home for social media. It was also not clear whose responsibility social media is in the institution—the library, information systems or communications? The paper observes that people feel they may be missing things that are outside a confined space, such as the library, as opposed to a borderless body of knowledge (Google). Further, the social media is all about doing-it-themselves and collaborating directly. In conclusion the paper observes that the advent of social media was unlikely to have an influence or impact on library functions in any major way, other than possibly negatively, by decoupling university libraries even further from scholarly information communication and provision.(Adopted from source document).

O'Dell, S. (2010). Opportunities and obligations for libraries in a social networking age: A survey of web 2.0 and networking sites. *Journal of Library Administration,* 50(3), 237-251. This paper focuses on the need to understand the emerging technologies and their relation to the collaboration of researchers and dissemination of scientific research. The author reviews available and upcoming software technologies that promote collaboration among scientists, the role of the library in informing the campus community about latest developments, and the opportunities for collaboration among librarians and scientists. The author points out the barriers that confront scientists in using Web.2 technologies and concerns such as commercialization of research results, lack of open access to scientific literature, and dearth of channels of communication for publicizing the results. O'Dell describes recent developments in promoting open access to scientific literature such as efforts of various bodies such as National Science Foundation and National Institutes of Health, and presents the current use of Web 2.0 technologies by researchers and librarians. The author outlines the impact of social media with examples. This paper lists various Web 2.0 tools and networking sites that help scientists to manage and share information to communicate and develop networks with other scientists.

Oleck, J. (2007). Libraries use MySpace to attract teens: More and more libraries are taking advantage of the popular social networking site. *School Library Journal,* 53 (7), 16-16. This is a news item mentioning that a growing number of libraries are using the social networking site MySpace to attract teenage patrons in U.S. and Canada with complete with eye-catching banners, animation, and sound effects. The article gives the example of two such libraries, the Sunnyside Regional Library in Fresno, California with a MySpace page hosting a 10-minute documentary explaining why parents should not fear the site, and the Hennepin County

(Minnesota) Library, (Minnesota) whose MySpace page helps students working on assignments. This article also reports the views of a couple of librarians mentioning how teenage patrons are using MySpace for sending messages. Another librarian reports that other libraries regularly seek her advice about how to set up a MySpace page and get approval from higher-ups. The author says that although MySpace has been getting a bad reputation for attracting online predators, libraries nationwide are using the popular site to their advantage.

Park, J. (2010). Differences among university students and faculties in social Networking site perception and use: Implications for academic library services. *The Electronic Library,* 28(3), 417-431. This paper aims at studying the usages of social networking sites by different university users and their perceptions. The study examines a site called Cyworld which, according to the author, is the most proliferated social network site in South Korea, penetrating deeply into people's lives, and 90 percent of South Koreans. He collects data through semi-structured and open-ended interviews conducted with undergraduates, graduates and faculty members at Yonsei University in Seoul, South Korea and analyzes the data by three different groups - undergraduates, graduates, and faculty members. He says that the findings demonstrated distinct patterns of social networking sites use. He says that although undergraduates used the profile service more than the community service, graduates used the community more than the profile service. Further, he says that faculty members were not active users. He lists six different factors which affect the usage patterns: desire for expression, peer influences, familiarity with information technologies, and sensitivity to privacy, nature of using the internet, and perception of social media. He asks for a differentiated approach for SNS-based academic library services

Parker, L. (2008). Second life: The seventh face of the library? *Program: Electronic Library and Information Systems,* 42(3), 232-242. This article aims at providing an introduction to SecondLife and outlines the involvement of a librarian in using SecondLife and the issues with which it is confronted. In this study the author attempts to clarify whether library activities in Second Life are different from library services in the real world, and observes that Second Life is just another "face" of the library. Based on personal experience, the findings of the study indicate that the SecondLife is still in the evolving stages of development, and is confronted with various barriers and challenges to overcome before it can be used widely within universities. However, this article shows that Second Life does provide an opportunity to experiment and explore what information resources are required in this environment, and how librarianship and librarians need to evolve to cater for users in a three dimensional world.

Penzhorn, C., & Pienaar, H. (2009). The use of social networking tools for innovative service delivery at the university of Pretoria library. *Innovation,* (38), 66-77. The article states that the social network tools have an impact on the scholarly activities of staff, faculty, and students in many ways. It says that the quality of service provided to its patrons depend to a large extent on the quality of service delivered by its reference librarians. The authors observe that the failure of the reference staff at the University of Pretoria Library to use the Web 2.0/Library 2.0 tools caused concern about the quality of service provided. Library management, they say, consequently decided to launch a program to encourage the implementation of Web 2.0/Library 2.0 tools in the library, and to ensure the sustainability of the initiatives. This article discusses the first phase of a collaborative project between the Library and the Department of Information Science with the aim of monitoring the introduction and the use of social networking services by the library reference staff, and the use of the tools by their clients. These collaborative units say that they have obtained valuable information on the range of products implemented as well as problems accompanying this, which has led to renewed strategies for addressing the shortcomings.

Powers, A. C., Schmidt, J., & Hill, C. (2008). Why can't we be friends? The MSU libraries find friends on Facebook. *Mississippi Libraries,* 72(1), 3-5. This article reviews the Facebook web site of Mississippi State University Libraries and describes the background and process of adoption of Facebook. The authors observe that public service departments had concerns with maintaining good communication with student workers regarding schedule adjustments. They say furthermore that, in order to provide more tools to library staff for responding to the changing needs of the university community, the Library 2.0 committee formed to provide staff training, to investigate emerging technologies, and recommended Facebook, after experimenting with it using invitees to a test page. The success of the closed group resulted in creating a public group for MSU libraries. The article states that the MSU Libraries Facebook page includes links to library services, an interactive discussion board; a "wall" that library staff use to post news, information about workshops; forthcoming events; connecting to the Ask-A-Librarian; connecting to the online catalog, databases, research guide, interlibrary loan, digital archive searching, RSS feeds; and links to the libraries' podcasts.

Rivero, V. (2010). Libraries get social -- social media, that is! *MultiMedia & Internet@Schools,* 17(6), 8-12. This article emphasizes the need for school libraries to adapt to the social media revolution that has taken place in the 21$^{st}$ century as reflected in iPhone apps, blogs, Nings, Facebook pages, and other social networking tools, sites, and platforms. The author is critical of schools in the United States which ban social media to protect young students from cyber bullying and for security reasons. The article stresses the benefits of social media usage in and around school libraries and encourages the teacher librarian/ media specialist to consider leading that charge. This article provides examples of school libraries that have reconciled with the virtual world and leveraged the social media revolution by the use of remote searches of school library/media center databases. The author outlines several social media software packages and applications for libraries, including AccessMyLibrary School Edition from Gale, Destiny

Library Manager from Follett Software, and the library automation solutions from TLC and provides a partial list of some major library automation companies that many libraries may find useful.

Rod-Welch, L. J. (2012). Incorporation and visibility of reference and social networking tools on ARLmember libraries' websites. *Reference Services Review,* 40(1), 138-171. This article presents the findings of a content analysis of 125 ARL library websites in North America to identify whether they incorporate reference and social networking tools in their library's website. For the purpose of this study, the author defines reference tools as the sources that the library users utilize to help them with their research needs. The 12 items considered for this study include live chat, e-mail/ask a librarian, research consultation/subject specialist/services, text/Short Message Service (SMS), telephone calls, YouTube,, Flicker, RSS feedback, Facebook, Twitter, Feedback suggestion, and 24/7 live chat. The author looks at which of these tools appear on the homepage, analyzes the data and presents the results. He concludes that while all the ARL libraries studied incorporate these tools to some extent in their libraries' websites, their presence is less visible on homepage in comparison to their presence elsewhere on their website.

Sachs, D. E., Eckel, E. J., & Langan, K. A. (2011). Striking a balance: Effective use of Facebook in an academic library. *Internet Reference Services Quarterly,* 16(1), 35. This article focuses on the background and progression that has gone through the adaption of Facebook at Western Michigan University Libraries. The authors state that they designed a survey that aimed at measuring the effectiveness of Facebook as a marketing, reference, and instruction tool as well as ensuring user comfort and satisfaction with a library's presence on Facebook and MySpace. 136 users at the university were surveyed. The survey noticed the student population heavily concentrated on Facebook, while the MySpace registered page with no traffic. The findings reveal that the majority of respondents found Facebook to be a useful site to learn about library resources and services. The authors mention that the results of this study indicate that the library Facebook page must maintain a balance between useful information and patron privacy. The article refers to data from another survey of 14 peer institutions and says that survey places Western Michigan University within the context of their peers' use of Facebook. The survey of peer institutions concludes that most libraries use Facebook for marketing and outreach purposes

Scale, M. (2008). Facebook as a social search engine and the implications for libraries in the twenty-first century. *Library Hi Tech*, 26(4), 540-556. This article aims at exploring the concept of social search, and the performance of Facebook as a social search engine, in order to understand the relationship between social networking sites (SNS) and social search. The author reviews the literature on social networking sites with special reference to Facebook and the concept of social search. He interprets 'social search' as human intermediary search and explores

Facebook as a social search engine through participant observation, personal experience and experimentation. The article states that the experiment is based on two identified search queries: To find an expert or experts in the English language using Facebook search features, and to locate information about a doctoral program in library and information science through group contacts. The findings, the author states, indicate that Facebook when utilized as a people search engine, yields irrelevant results in response to search queries for unknown persons or groups. Facebook may also fail to provide timely and relevant results when attempting to get information from persons with whom the user has a weak relationship. This is a well-researched paper highlighting the concept of social search.

Schultz-Jones, B. A., & Ledbetter, C. E. (2009). Building relationships in the school social network: Science teachers and school library media specialists report key dimensions. *School Libraries Worldwide,* 15(2), 23-48. This paper reports research results from a 2008 study of the social networks of school library media specialists (SLMS) in north Texas and a 2007/2008 survey of science teacher attitudes towards SLMS in north Texas. Analytic methodologies included social network analysis, statistical analysis, and qualitative content analysis of interviews. Analyses of the results suggest that two key dimensions may provide a foundation for building relationships in the school social network: credibility and visibility. These dimensions may provide opportunities to strengthen the collaboration efforts between SLMS and science teachers. Future research will include proposals to develop collaboration skills and measure the impact of these efforts on student science achievement. With a national emphasis in the United States on requisite science literacy skills, efforts to strengthen cross-disciplinary collaboration skills and opportunities should yield positive results (Author abstract). This survey did not focus on any of the social networking sites

Secker, J. (2008). Case study 5: Libraries and Facebook. *Libraries and Social Software in Education.* Available at: http://clt.Lse.Ac.uk/Projects /Case_Study_Five_report. Pdf This case study explores the use of the social networking site Facebook as a tool for libraries and librarians in a UK scenario. The author says that it was largely based on the literature and experiences of the project team, libraries and librarians using the site. The report observes certain key concerns expressed by librarians using Facebook, such as appropriateness of using social spaces for professional activities, privacy and security issues, and commercial nature of the site. The report mentions several library related Facebook applications such as JSTOR Search, LibGuides Librarian, Facebook Librarian, Books, iRead, Bookshare, COPAC Search, European Library Search, World Cat Search, UIUC Library catalog, and other library searches. The report recommends several suggestions for best practice for using Facebook as a librarian

Sekyere, K. (2009). Too much hullabaloo about Facebook in libraries! is it really helping libraries? *Nebraska Library Association Quarterly,* 40(2), 25-27. This author describes the social network site Facebook and says it offers an increasingly large range of applications and functions to users. However, he questions the extent of the use of the site by students in interacting with librarians. He looks at whether the service is seen as helpful or somewhat disturbing to students. He states that many of the services provided by libraries on Facebook have very low use in reality. He observes that the students typically turn to Facebook to have fun, not to do research or any academic work and often they login to Facebook as a way of taking a break from academic work, many seeing it as invading their personal digital space. Citing a survey conducted in 2008 on students and information technology, the author states that 9 to 10 percent of students place access restrictions on their profiles. He says that when the first step of making students 'friends' of Facebook is not achieved, the question of students accepting it becomes a big challenge to libraries. He observes that many students are likely to be hesitant and uncomfortable in accepting faculty and librarians as Facebook friends primarily because of privacy issues. He suggests that libraries should focus on ways to deliver library service thru mobile devices.

*Sharing, privacy and trust in our networked world [OCLC - reports]* Retrieved 2/26/2012, from http://www.oclc.org/reports/sharing/ This OCLC report aimed at studying the use of social networking sites and other social media on the Web, how and what users and librarians share on the Web, related privacy issues, opinions on online privacy, and the role of librarians in social networking. Based on a survey of the general public from six countries and of library managers, this report provides valuable information on the use of social networking by library users. The report, categorized into 9 sections, focuses on various aspects of social network including social spaces, privacy, security and trust, libraries and social networking. The appendixes to this report provide very useful information and data on students, readings and other sources. The section on social networking and libraries highlights the public opinion and states that the public respondents surveyed do not currently see a role for libraries in their new social networked world. In addition, it appears that, like the public, U.S. library directors do not see a role for social networking in libraries. Although this report is based on a survey from the general public from six developed countries - Canada, France, Germany, Japan, the United Kingdom and the United States—and of library directors from the U.S, the findings of the report would equally hold good for other countries where the social networking phenomenon is in use.

Spomer, M. Y. (2008). The Fine Art of Throwing Sheep: How Facebook Can Contribute to Librarianship and Community at Theological Institutions. *Theological Librarianship*, 1(1), 10-21. This informative essay describes the origin, development, and salient features of Facebook. It presents the way Facebook can contribute to librarianship and community at various theological institutions in the U.S. It says that for theological librarians, Facebook could serve as a potential tool to connect with individuals and create community as well as serving as a marketing and reference tool. It points out that Facebook maintains an 85% market share of 4-year U.S. universities. It depicts Facebook as a service which belongs in a wider category of social networking services which aimed for a much more diverse user base. The author says that Facebook's biggest contribution to community is its capacity to help users discover and know people in ways that they feel are important, and on their own terms since the profiles allow people to express interests, beliefs, and talents that may not be apparent in face-to-face interaction. This article lists several useful references and library sites.

Sokoloff, J. (2009). International libraries on Facebook. *Journal of Web Librarianship,* 3(1), 75-80. This author says that because of the popularity of online social networking on the Web, organizations launched sites such as Orkut by Google Inc. and MSAN Spaces by Microsoft Inc, and that in this arena, Facebook has become the world's most popular social networking Web site. Recognizing the use and growth of number of users of Facebook, the world's most popular social networking Web site, he says that academic and public libraries worldwide have adopted it and he offers examples of both promising strategies and challenges in their execution of Facebook pages. This article looks at the efforts of some libraries outside the United States. They are: University of Portsmouth Library, United Kingdom; University Of Pretoria Library Services, South Africa; Cacak Public Library, Serbia; Yarra Plenty Regional Library Service, Melbourne, Australia; Manchester Library & Information Service, United Kingdom; and Toronto Public Library, Ontario, Canada. The author observes that the social networks have the potential to increase globalization and says that it will be important to lift our eyes beyond just one country's borders and continue to explore the international landscape.

Starr, J. (2010). California Digital Library in twitter-Land. *Computers in Libraries*, 30(7), 23-27. This is an anecdotal paper about the author's experience as the manager of the California Digital Library (CDL) with the implementation of Twitter service as a communication channel. Noticing that many archivists and teachers were using Twitter and that this pattern was emerging for several other CDL programs as well, the author observes that a central CDL account could serve as a key coordinating role to get CDL's news and ideas out to a wider audience. The project was launched and implemented with a threefold objective of gaining new readers for the newsletter CDLINFO, to amplify the voices and messages of the accounts, and to increase CDL's visibility in consistence with CDL's values of openness and sharing. The author observes that many people use Twitter with mobile devices, and others read the content stream using Twitter "dashboard" tools such as TweetDeck or HootSuite. In order to assess the account's performance, this service depends on information sources such as website statistics and tracking the number of followers of @CalDigLib over time.

Thornton, L. (2009). Facebook for libraries. *Christian Librarian,* 52(3), 112-115. This is an introductory article delineating salient features of the social networking site Facebook, one of the most popular online social networking sites to emerge in the twenty-first century available to all users, regardless of affiliation. This author describes the origin, development, popularity, and use of this tool among the student community and its logical adaption, increasingly so, by libraries. The author says that this tool is well suited for a variety of academic purposes in libraries to reach patrons. The possible uses include information literacy and networking with persons inside and outside primary networks. The article cites extensively from other authors and discusses their perceptions of their use of Facebook. The author states that students generally respond more rapidly to a message sent in Facebook than to one sent via e-mail. He says that Facebook increases the library's visibility and students' awareness of new databases, services, and resources of interest to them. This article is very useful for an introduction to Facebook.

Torres-Salinas, D., Cabezas-Clavijo, Á., Ruiz-Pérez, R., & López-Cózar, E. D. (2011). State of the library and information science blogosphere after social networks boom: A metric approach. *Library & Information Science Research,* 33(2), 168-174. The authors of this article researched the impact of the Web 2.0 tool blogosphere on social networking sites such as Facebook, MySpace, and Twitter after they gained popularity. They made a metric analysis of blogs on library and information science (LIS) between November 2006 and June 2009 that were indexed on the Libworm search engine and they analyzed the data quantitatively. LibWorm search engine is a professional development tool and a current awareness tool for people who work in libraries or care about libraries (www.libworm.com). The authors state they have analyzed 1108 personal and corporate blogs with a total of 275,103 posts to calculate survival rate, production, and visibility via such indicators as links received using Technorati authority and Google's PagePank. They found a 52% decrease in the number of active blogs over the study period. The paper concludes that the emergence of such platforms as Facebook and Twitter appears to have impacted both personal and corporate blogs in losing their prominence.

Trainor, C. (2010). Will social media activism reverse the fortunes of besieged libraries? *American Libraries,* 41 (5), 18. This article highlights the role of social networking sites such as Facebook and Twitter in serving libraries, not only for marketing library and information services, but also for lobbying the cause of libraries in times of financial crisis. The author states that in the United States social media campaigns have worked toward influencing decision makers when they attempted to close down some libraries or slash library budgets. He mentions that when the Charlotte Mecklenburg Library in North Carolina voted to close 12 branches and lay off more than 140 library employees in response to a $2 million cut, an online fund-raising and awareness campaign quickly spread across Facebook and Twitter to compensate for the budget hole. Although that target was not met, he says, the campaign forced trustees to rescind the closures and instead they decided to reduce hours and layoffs. He recalls other similar online campaigns that occurred in Los Angeles, California and Boston, Massachusetts. Apparently, social media is in an advantageous position for more rapid and widespread coverage about impending crises.

Topper, E. F. (2007). Social networking in libraries. *New Library World,* 108 (7-8), 378-380. With a view to examine the impact of social networking on public and academic libraries, this paper reviews the literature and comments on it. Based on observation by one of the authors of the cited papers, it states that the librarians use their preferred method of communication. The author cites Pew Internet Study and estimates that MySpace is being used by between 80 and 90 million plus users in public libraries followed by Facebook in academic libraries. The author says that after school, teenagers flock to libraries to use social network sites, making the computer areas into vibrant social places and at the same time forcing the librarians to find ways to accommodate teens and to provide sufficient access for students to do research papers. The author points out issues that include personal safety, monitoring for content, and the relationship between institutional missions and a new generation's expectations of privacy. Topper emphasizes the value of planning to find the ways patrons access information.

Users don't expect social networking from libraries. (2008). *Research Information,* (34), 12. This paper highlights the findings of Harris Interactive online surveys in 2007 http://www.oclc.org/reports/sharing and (http://www.oclc.org/reports/pdfs/sharing_part2.pdf for the report on behalf of OCLC. This OCLC study reveals that just 13 percent of the public feels it is the role of the library to create a social networking site for their communities. The top reasons provided by general-public respondents for why the library should not build a social networking site included: 'library is for learning/ information' (25 per cent), 'not the role of the library' (16 per cent) and 'library is not for socializing' (seven per cent). The report also states that the Internet is familiar territory, with 89 percent of respondents having been online for four years or more and nearly 25 percent having used the Internet for more than ten years. It states further that more than a quarter of the general public respondents currently participate in some type of social media or social networking site and half of the college students surveyed use social sites. However, the percentage of Internet users that have used a library Web site has decreased since OCLC's last study.

Wan, G. ((2011). How academic libraries reach users on Facebook. *College & Undergraduate Libraries*, 18(4), 307-318. This article gives a brief introduction to Facebook and its salient features and popularity trends among the student community in terms of percentage of users. The author examines the Facebook presence of Association of Research Libraries (ARL) member institutions, analyzing it in terms of launch time and success trend in reaching out to users. He identifies a total number of 159 active pages from ARL libraries by searching the Facebook pages with its default search engine which allows search through all profiles, pages, and groups, and by means of Google advance search.

He says that the majority of libraries maintain at least one Facebook page focusing mostly library events and resource updates. Overall, the author says that the numbers of Fans are not impressive as the number varied from six to 2280, with a median of 136. Concerning updates, the author observes that most libraries do not post on their pages very often and that the majority of library Facebook pages are not successful in attracting Fans.

Watt, I. (2010). Changing visions of parliamentary libraries: From the enlightenment to Facebook. *IFLA Journal,* 36(1), 47-60. The author, Iain Watt, who works for the Library of the European Parliament, observes that the parliamentary library is based on the ideals of the Enlightenment: to serve a curious and well-informed Member who uses reason and science to hold the executive to account and to contribute on legislative and policy issues. However, he says that this vision of the 1800s when the parliamentary library was born is no longer valid. He says that the executive has grown in scale and in scope, covering many more issues in which policy choices and consequences are complex. The populations represented are more numerous. Information has increased in volume, turnover, and diversity of format and channel. As such, he suggests that rather than focusing on quality of information produced/delivered, parliamentary libraries should focus on quality of information actually used. Improving ease of access to information and focusing on specialist Parliamentary libraries must also take into consideration the growth in Members' support staff and adapt their marketing to a business-to-business model. A focus on core competencies and their deployment in new areas of parliamentary information work is one vision for the future. The two citations from this paper are worth noting while discussing the role of parliamentary libraries in modern times. "Congress usually does not apply scientific knowledge in the making of public policy because: first, members of Congress are more interested in adopting policies that will help them get re-elected than policies that conform to standards of rationality and efficiency". "Policy-oriented research… does not compel legislators to adopt a certain alternative because research findings are often ambiguous, inconclusive, incongruous and even contradictory to other research findings". (Adopted from source document).

Webb, P. (2007). Prevailing practices for libraries on MySpace. *College and Undergraduate Libraries,* 14(2), 39-44. This author studies various styles of the social network site MySpace in academic libraries in order find common types of information and style to attract and inform patrons to the library. The study mentions the availability of a variety of template designs to experiment to find out what best suits their needs. He observes that the majority of libraries did not deviate from the standard format provided by MySpace, although MySpace has the unique feature of allowing creators to completely change and modify the layout of their personal MySpace page. He concludes that by using free MySpace template sites such as CreateBlog.com, libraries can develop their own unique style to attract, service their patrons, and connect with new audiences. The author mentions that in all the libraries viewed, blogs were either consistently used or not used at all and says that the blogs were mostly treated as another way of distributing study guides or general library information.

Widows, K. (2009). Web 2.0 moves 2.0 quickly 2.0 wait: setting up a library Facebook presence at the University of Warwick. *SCONUL Focus,* (46), 54-59. The author says that several libraries in England such as the Bodleian law library have adopted social networking tools for providing library services. In this article, he discusses how Facebook is used in the library and information services of the University of Warwick (UW) in Warwickshire, England. The author states that UW decided to establish a Facebook page, after they had observed that students often use it. He says that the university still considers the terms and conditions in setting up the Facebook page including the issues of student social space encroachment. This article describes briefly how the project was initiated, the process of planning, implementation, and servicing. He states that UW's application of the web technology helped them reach their target audience and also provided the university with an effective communication tool. He observes that Facebook has made significant changes to various aspects of its service several times ever since the page was launched in 2007. The author acknowledges the team effort of all involved in the implementation of the project.

Weiter, S. (2008). Who's REALLY computer savvy? Web 2.0 technologies and your library. *Legal Information Management,* 8(4), 270-273. The author, Stephen Weiter, raises certain basic questions, such as: Who is using Web 2.0? What are we using it for? Are "Gen X-ers/Gen Y-ers" more computer savvy in changing environment? Do "Baby Boomers" (born between 1946 and 1964) fear change and rely too much on email? He attempts to answer these questions. Based on various sources, he says that Web 2.0 is a living term describing changing trends in the use of World Wide Web technology and web design that aims to enhance creativity, information sharing, collaboration and functionality of the web. He questions the assumption that older librarians are afraid of change, or that they are less savvy than their younger counterparts and says they are changing and embracing change all the time by adopting emerging technologies and gadgets persistently. He cites Nielsen/Netratings's data and states that there are 78 million American "Baby-boomers" online out of 208 million total US users, 144 million of whom can be considered active users. He says that he uses social network tools such as Facebook, Ning, LinkedIn, Flickr, Library Thing, Google, and Yahoo and participates in blogs, wikis, podcasts, and uses SMS messaging regularly and identifies himself as a law librarian on each of these sites where he has a profile. Yet very little, if any, of his communications on these sites is with library patrons. He believes that his pattern of working might hold well with other librarians and they too are exploring the possibilities of adopting these tools in their organizations. However, he says that a multiplicity of tools and options is not conducive to productivity all the time. This is very thought-provoking article.

Xia, D. Z. (2009). Marketing library services through Facebook groups. *Library Management,* 30(6/7), 469-477. This article emphasizes that there is a greater need for marketing of academic library services to students and faculty by resorting to social networking tools. The need for this marketing is even greater in view of the availability of search engines such as Google.com and yahoo.com which have altered the role of libraries by offering students easier ways to discover research materials online and cutting the necessity of physically visiting a library. In order to find the suitability of Facebook groups for marketing of library services, the author conducts a survey at two major universities in the United States and analyzes the results in comparison with two global Facebook groups. The findings reported indicate that the success of Facebook Groups is controlled by the active organization of librarians and by using more general topics to keep discussions alive. He says that by effectively organizing Facebook groups, libraries can extend their services to more users targeting faculty and staff in addition to students in support of their research and teaching. A critique of this article appears at Haglund, L., & Herron, D. (2010). Research into the impact of Facebook as a library marketing tool is inconclusive. *Evidence Based Library & Information Practice, 5*(3), 56-58

Agosto, D. E., & Abbas, J. (2011). *Teens, libraries, and social networking: What librarians need to know* Santa Barbara, Calif: Libraries Unlimited. The editors of this collection of articles, Denise Agosto and June Abbas, strongly believe that teens and young adults (YA) are largest group in terms of numbers in using social networking sites, with the majority of them connecting with their friends, friends of friends, and so on via these social media. The editors state that public libraries can benefit from their use in three major ways: by broadening the reach of the library's young adult programs and services by enabling the library to better support teens' healthy social development, and by facilitating opportunities for public librarians to teach teens how to engage in safer online interactions. This book focuses on ten major topics, including using the social network sites to connect teens to YA literature, legislative issues, safety/privacy issues, and the social and educational benefits of social networking. The authors of various chapters explain how these issues can impact library services to young adults and offer suggestions and steps that will help librarians utilize social networking tools to enhance library services to teens. The book is educational and valuable as a general reading as well as a practicum tool for librarians.

Berube, L. (2011). *Do you Web 2.0? : Public libraries and social networking.* Oxford: Chandos. Although the subtitle of this book reads as *public libraries and social networking*, the book addresses Web 2.0 tools such as RSS, podcasts, Weblogs, micro-blogs, flicker, wikis, folksonomies, social bookmarking, tagging, and social catalogs and not social networking sites such as Facebook and MySpace. The author says that many of Web 2.0 tools used to facilitate sociability on their own are incorporated into social network services to build or attract communities. The book discusses a bit of UK public library pre-history, experimentation with Web 2.0, and couple of case studies of blogs. She reviews Web 2.0 tools and provides practical advice and case studies on how they can be applied in the public libraries.

Landis, C. (2010). *Social Networking Primer for Librarians*. New York: Neal-Schuman Publishers. This book provides a basic understanding of tools and techniques for using social networking sites such as Facebook, MySpace, Friendster, and others. The author, Cliff Landis, states that this primer is aimed at helping librarians of all types of libraries to strengthen user-library connections. It also covers the policies and privacy applications of social network sites to enable librarians to make informed decisions by protecting privacy and intellectual property. Chapter one provides basics, definitions, characteristics, and the origin and evolution of social network sites. Chapter 2 gives tips in choosing the site and lists the possible services one would like to offer in the chosen space. The next chapter explains creation of MySpace and Facebook accounts and their applications. Chapter 4 discusses marketing plans, library brand identity, and the creation of a social marketing campaign. Chapter 5 describes friending etiquettes, use of proper language, and content. The last section provides tips on monitoring usage statistics, conducting surveys, creating focus groups, and setting up of goals for the site. Additionally, the author provides a glossary of terms and selected sites, as well as a listing of recommended reading. Presented in a simple and non-technical language, this book, as stated by the author, is an excellent resource for librarians intending to increase their library's online presence and to strengthen the library-user connection through online social networks.

Lupa, R. M. (2009). *More than MySpace: Teens, librarians, and social networking*. Santa Barbara, Calif: Libraries Unlimited. This book is aimed at Young Adult Service librarians in order to equip themselves with skills and knowledge of social networking tools whereby they can better attract young people and teens to the public library to gather, communicate, and connect. This is a collection of articles presenting different views of ideas by a student, a teacher, a teen librarian, a technology guru, and others. The focal point of this book is that social networks can be used for study groups, homework help, and school/library partnerships, with students participating as creators of content rather than mere users. As a prelude to various chapters, the author examines the social networking phenomenon, the what, and why of it, the history of networking, the use of sites by teens, and application to public libraries. The final chapter gives anecdotes from a national survey of librarians concerning social networking. Along with the useful ideas presented in this volume, the author provides a glossary describing salient features of the top twenty social networking sites at one place.

Solomon, L. (2011). *Doing social media so it matters: A librarian's guide*. Chicago: American Library Association. Chicago: American Library Association.

The author states that this book is aimed at people who are already familiar with the major social networking tools such as Twitter, Facebook, and MySpace, and are interested in using these and other tools better. The book focuses on how a library should plan to use social media and to manage interactions. The author offers practical information on how to get the library staff and management to accept and use social media tools. Divided into seven chapters, the book starts with an overview of how to get the library staff involved. The second chapter describes setting goals and comparing social media sites and choosing the sites .The next two chapters describe social capital and strategies for success. The book provides several do's and don'ts with specific examples on making status updates for interacting with followers and friends. Chapter 5 discusses the measurement of the use of social media by means of opinion gathering, and by monitoring positive press, YouTube views, blog comments, retweets, number of visitors, and number of friends/fans/followers. Chapter 6, entitled "Is it worth it?" discusses positive and negative sides of the site as well as problems and prospects. The author encourages librarians to set measurable targets and recommends approaches to "pulling the plug" if it is found that social media are not working for your library. This book is useful for people who already possess a proficiency in using social media sites.

# Title Index

## A



## B



## C



## D

## E



## F



## G



## H



## I



## L

## T



## U



## W

# AUTHOR'S INDEX

# LIST OF PERIODICALS COVERED

Access (1204-0472), 14(2), 21-23
Against the Grain, 19(3), 86-87
Alabama Librarian, 58(1), 8-11
American Libraries, 39(7), 32; 40(12), 35-35; 41 (5), 18; 42(5), 42-45
Behavioral & Social Sciences Librarian, 27(2), 116-118
Business Information Review, 26(1), 57-58
Choice, 44(12), 2011-2021
Christian Librarian, 52(3), 112-115
College & Research Libraries News, 71(1), 10-12, 24; 72(1), 79-90
College and Undergraduate Libraries, 14(2), 39-44; 18(4), 307-318.
Community & Junior College Libraries, 16(2), 100-113.
Computers in Libraries, 27(8), 18-22; 27(8), 30-32; 29(5), 17-18; 29(9), 29-31; 30(7), 23-27; 27(10), 46
CQ Researcher, 16(27), 641
Doing social media so it matters: A librarian's guide (Book)
ELearn, 2010(10), 7.
The Electronic Library, 28(3), 417-431
IFLA Journal, 36(1), 47-60.
Impact: Journal of the Career Development Group, 12 (4), 96-97
Information Outlook, 14(7), 9-12.
Information Technology & Libraries, 26(1), 23-34; 26 (1), 23
Information Today, 28(2), 14-15; 28(6), 1, 31-2
Innovation, (38), 66-77
International Leads, 24(4), 5
Internet Reference Services Quarterly, 13(1), 15-55; 13(1), 69-85; 16(1), 35

Journal of Academic Librarianship, 373-375
Journal of Electronic Resources in Medical Libraries, 5(2), 123-132
Journal of Electronic Resources Librarianship, 20(4), 205-209
Journal of Library Administration, 47(3-4), 191-209; 50(3), 237-251
The Journal of Academic Librarianship, 373-375
Journal of the Medical Library Association, 97(1), 43-46.
Journal of Web Librarianship, 1(2), 71-74; 3(1), 75-80; 3(2), 111-128; 4(4), 333-350
Knowledge Quest, 36(2), 34-37
Legal Information Management, 8(4), 270-273; 9(3), 175-181
Library & Information Science Research, 33(2), 168-174
Library Hi Tech News, 24(8), 30-32; 25(4), 5-7; 26(4), 540-556
Library Journal, 131(15), 32
Library Management, 30(6/7), 469-477
Library of Congress Information Bulletin, 69(5), 84-86
Library Technology Reports, 46(8), 34-37
Medical Reference Services Quarterly, 29 (1), 75-84; 30(3), 233-244
Mississippi Libraries, 72(1), 3-5
MultiMedia & Internet@Schools, 17(6), 8-12; 15(5), 27-29; 16(5), 28-31
Multimedia Information and Technology, 36(4), 20-21
Nebraska Library Association Quarterly, 40(2), 25-27
New Library World, 108 (7-8), 378-380; 111(11-12), 468-479
NextSpace, (7), 12-13
Online (Weston, Conn.), 33(5), 35-37
Pennsylvania Library Association Bulletin, 63(6), 8-10
Portal: Libraries and the Academy, 9(1), 25-36
Program: Electronic Library and Information Systems, 42(3), 232-242
Public Libraries, 48(3), 32-37; 23(3), 6-8
Public Library Journal, 23(3), 6-8
Public Services Quarterly, 4(4), 353-365; 5(3), 208-211; 7(3-4), 102-110
Reference Services Review, 40(1), 138-171
Research Information, (34), 12
Scandinavian Public Library Quarterly. pp. 18-19
School Libraries Worldwide, 15(2), 23-48
School Library Journal, 53 (7), 16-16; 55(10), 44-46; 55(12), 17
SCONUL Focus, (46), 54-59; (48), 23-25; (49), 12-14
Searcher, 15(9)
Sharing, privacy and trust in our networked world [OCLC - reports]
SRELS Journal of Information Management, 47(3), 283-288

Technology, 3, (2) 50-54
Tennessee Libraries, 58(2), 1-3
Theological Librarianship, 1(1), 10-21
Webology, 3(2), 2006

# INDEX

**N**



**O**



**P**



**Q**



**R**

## S



## T



## U

## V



## W



## Y